# Three's A Crowd

**Trios that can be performed with any other combination of instruments within Junior Book A.**

# Saxophone

A mix and match collection of 30 trio arrangements by James Power.

CHESTER MUSIC
London/New York/Paris/Sydney/Copenhagen/Berlin/Madrid/Tokyo

T0058833

Exclusive distributors:
**Chester Music**
(a division of Music Sales Limited)
8/9 Frith Street, London W1D 3JB, England.

**Music Sales Corporation**
257 Park Avenue South, New York, NY 10010,
United States of America.

**Music Sales Pty Limited**
120 Rothschild Avenue, Rosebery, NSW 2018, Australia.

Order No. PM221563R
ISBN 0-7119-9389-0
This book © Copyright 2002 Chester Music.

Instruments featured on the cover provided by Macari's Musical Instruments, London.
Models provided by Truly Scrumptious and Norrie Carr.
Photography by George Taylor.
Cover design by Chloë Alexander.
Printed in the United Kingdom.

**Your Guarantee of Quality:**
As publishers, we strive to produce every book to the highest commercial standards.
The music has been freshly engraved and the book has been carefully designed to
minimise awkward page turns and to make playing from it a real pleasure.
Particular care has been given to specifying acid-free, neutral-sized paper made from
pulps which have not been elemental chlorine bleached. This pulp is from farmed
sustainable forests and was produced with special regard for the environment.
Throughout, the printing and binding have been planned to ensure a sturdy, attractive
publication which should give years of enjoyment.
If your copy fails to meet our high standards, please inform us and we will gladly replace
it or offer a refund.

Music Sales' complete catalogue describes thousands of titles and is available in
full colour sections by subject, direct from Music Sales Limited.
Please state your areas of interest and send a cheque/postal order for £1.50 for postage
to: Music Sales Limited, Newmarket Road, Bury St Edmunds, Suffolk IP33 3YB.

**www.musicsales.com**

# Contents

# Lavender Blue

Traditional

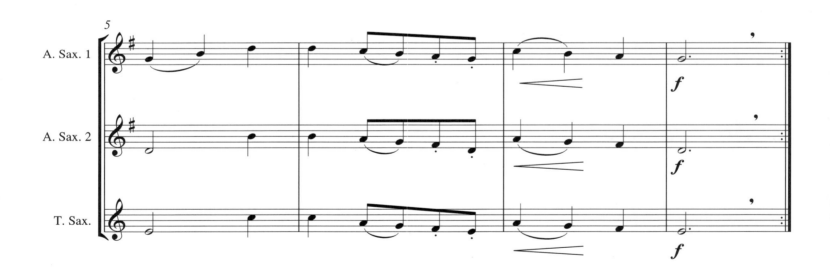

# Little Brown Jug

Traditional

Con Moto

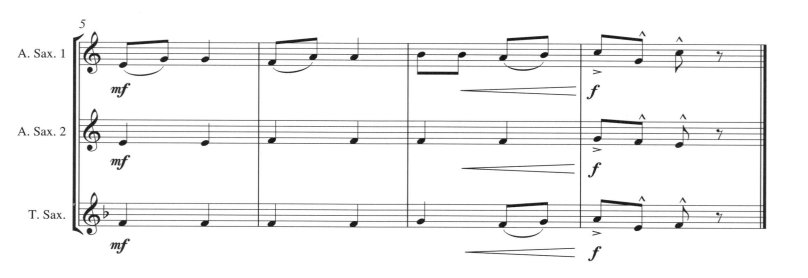

# Twinkle Twinkle Little Star

Traditional

# Clementine

Traditional

# Sur le Pont d'Avignon

French Traditional

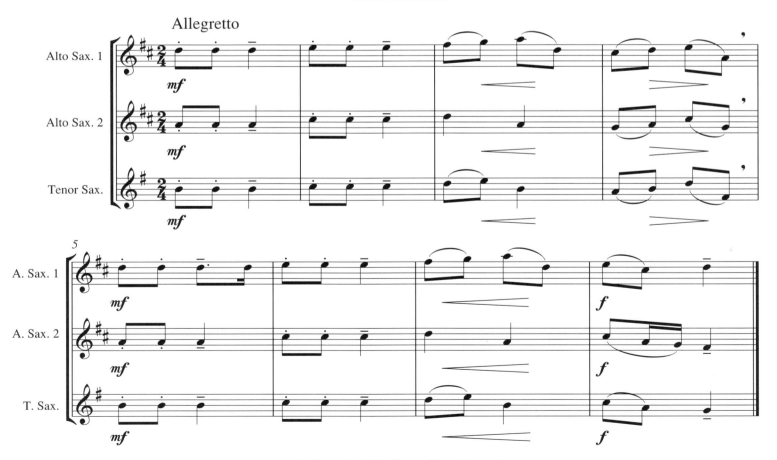

# London Bridge Is Falling Down

Traditional

# Old MacDonald

Traditional

# Kum Ba Yah

Traditional

# Go Down Moses

Spiritual

# Looby Loo

Traditional

# Au Clair de la Lune

French Traditional

# Skip To My Lou

Traditional

# This Old Man

Traditional

14

# The Run Around

James Power

15

# Big Rock Candy Mountain

Traditional

16

# Dance Of The Hours

A.Ponchielli

**Delicato**

# Aaron's Beard

James Power

Scherzando

# Yankee Doodle

Traditional

# Mairi's Wedding

Irish Traditional

20

# Li'l Liza Jane

Traditional

21

# Quartermaster's Stores

Traditional

# When Johnny Comes Marching Home

Traditional

# Yellow Bird

Traditional

# O Susanna

Traditional

# Early One Morning

Traditional

# How's Your Father

James Power

# Boston Belles

Traditional

# Snap

James Blackford

# Can Can

J. Offenbach

# The Highland Lassie

James Power